Against the Dark

Against the Dark

---

road poems

James Benger

Tyler Robert Sheldon

Stubborn Mule Press
Devil's Elbow, MO
stubbornmulepress.com

All poems copyright © 2018
James Benger and Tyler Robert Sheldon

First Edition 11 7 5 3 2 1
ISBN: 978-1-946642-80-6
LCCN: 2018913395
Design, edits and layout: Jason Ryberg, Jeanette Powers
stubbornmulepress@gmail.com @stubbornmulepress
Cover Image: Alex Arceneaux

All rights reserved. No part of this publication may be reproduced or transmitted in any form or by any means, electronic or mechanical, including photocopying, recording or by info retrieval system, w/out prior written permission from the author. Brief passages quoted for review purposes are permitted.

Also by James Benger:
jamesbengerauthor@gmail.com
  Little Fires Hiding (with Jason Baldinger)
    (Kung Fu Treachery Press, 2018)
  You've Heard It All Before (GigaPoem, 2017)
  As I Watch You Fade (EMP, 2016)

Also by Tyler Robert Sheldon:
TylerRobertSheldon.com
  Consolation Prize (Finishing Line Press, 2018)
  Driving Together (Meadowlark Books, 2018)
  Traumas (Yellow Flag Press, 2017)
  First Breaths of Arrival (Oil Hill Press, 2016)

JB

Thanks to Tyler, Prospero's Books, Jeanette Powers and Jason Ryberg at Stubborn Mule Press, Dad, Hannah, Milo and Felix.

TRS

Big thanks to the folks at Stubborn Mule Press, to my family, and to the significant folks who encourage my work, including Alex, Kevin, Denise, Caryn, Amy and Amy, Chris, Keagan, Trudy, and others. And thanks to James for inviting me to co-write this book.

"Where you've nothing else construct ceremonies out
of the air and breathe upon them."
— Cormac McCarthy

"At each fork, you must make a decision."
— C.S. Lewis

Contents

Voice	11
Outset	12
Running	13
Armadillo	14
Winners	15
First Gas Station	17
Rest Stop	18
Flat	19
Come on Down	20
Bus Stop	22
South Kansas, Late	24
Sometime After Midnight	25
Border Conversation	26
Expectations	27
Interior Monologue/Dessert	29
Christ of the Ozarks	31
Ravenden	33
Drops	34
Interior Monologue/Cancer	36
Silent Aftermath	37
Interior Monologue/Passenger	38
Goals	39
Just Past Midnight	40
Seat	41
Motel Pool	43
On the Take	44
4:15	46
Toward the End	48
Marker	49
Drive	50
Lights	51
Storm Warning	52
Drill	53
News	54
Wet	55
Return Ghazal	57

Voice

For a lot of people it hurts to talk,
not necessarily about the harder things,
but because of the action itself: air
out over the lining of the lungs, like
road. Up and up and out. And again.
Do this in a certain fashion
for the rest of your trafficked life.
Then vibrate. Not like guitar strings

to which the vocal chords aren't
even close, no matter who says so.
You must vibrate like a body
in the brand new cold. Your throat
must do this. No matter for how long.
You will find your voice behind
your smallest rock of self.
If done right, you won't need any help.

Outset

I wasn't so worried about the drive itself.
Midwestern roads at night risk deer and strangers,
hooves or thumbs darting from the road's dark edge
to tumble your plans down a hill you'd never seen coming.
This is why we decided to drive in shifts.

We'd eventually packed the car full of paper
and enough bottled water to stretch three weeks
and headed south from Kansas City.
We could find all the food we needed on the way—
enough gas stations between here and Louisiana
to compile an entire annotated encyclopedia
of roller grill taquitos. This is how writers
see the world: everything can be captured
with enough ink and enough time.

The first gas station wasn't for fifty miles.

Running

It seemed like a good enough idea
and rubber always smells good
leaving its mark on blacktop.

The coal black Mustang
was meant to be a loner,
but three years in,
that dream was long in the ground.

He had his supplies,
the paper I'd use,
I'd probably drink a water or two
along the way.
I had my provisions;
I hated I could only find room
for a few plastic bottles,
the brown,
the clear,
and in that pouch to hold
your keys
or wallet
or pencils,
the Ziploc bag
of what the dude swore
wasn't schwag.
I didn't plan on boasting the contraband,
but I wasn't going to hide it, neither.

My foot on the gas,
another bug on the glass.

Armadillo

Route 71 sends them out to keep drivers awake:
armored bolus of road, the armadillo plays
high-stakes pinball, tries to smash
what comes its way. Derek sees it first, too late,
blames the bag of schwag on his lap,
swerves the black Mustang. Like that baggie,
I don't know where he got this car.

We chew some road-edge gravel
until he wrenches us back to the blacktop.
Behind us in the mirror the armadillo coils,
then takes careful doomed aim
at another car.

Winners

Maybe the bag didn't help,
but that sumbitch had it out for me.

The radio had just begun to remind us
that she was a good girl,
loved all kinds of American apple pie stuff
(don't matter how baked you get,
still easily his worst song).

Little sucker just there
like some sacrifice,
like some cartoon damsel on the tracks.
I wrenched the wheel and missed him,
but we hit shoulder,
bald-ish tires threatening worse.
I kept my cool,
kept 'em at two and ten,
kept my eyes ahead,
kept the j. in my incisors.
Might've mumbled a smoky
"motherfucker,"
but who woudn't've?
Unaligned alignment fighting all the way,
I got the Mustang back on the black.
Every yellow dash flying by,
an almost heart attack.

Rex says something,
something cool and witty like he does,
but I hear the adrenaline waver.

I spit it to the night.
"Maybe that's the last for a while,"
I say to him,
to myself,

to the air.
I almost believe myself sometimes.

He offers to drive.
I say no,
but next piss break,
he's gonna press
and I won't fight it.

The armadillo's still alive
and so are we.
Sometimes ending it still breathing
is all you need to
call the day a win.

First Gas Station

The roller grills aren't so replete as I'd thought.
Yellow floor signs bar badly needed bathrooms.
Ahead of me a woman says *Six dollars?? What
do you think I am, a millionaire?* Her daughter,
small, puts back the pink plush monkey, pouts.

The pump ahead of ours is bagged. Gas is down
ten cents, not bad. My passenger is slumped,
asleep, seatbelt reddening his neck.
I keep pressure on a busted handle
and the numbers fold themselves
over into the tank, filling it up

just until the next station. I wish
for open bathrooms, open grills
and the sun dips a little over the fields
like others just ahead of us, another
mile marker away, another, and another still.

Rest Stop

Sometimes you wake up
and all you can think
is great lakes and long sighs.
I'm told I slept through the gas stop,
and that was probably for the best.

It's a mixed bag;

pissing out on the road,
highway wind chilling you,
directing the stream,
it's a kind of unbridled nature.
You feel more together
with your great-grandma on the rez,
or the coyote in the middle-distance
eyeing you,
wondering if you got food.

Or maybe you're just watering the grass.

But here in the disinfectant,
fluorescent wonderland of weary bodies,
I drink in the ammonia smell,
pelt the pink disc in the urinal,
and think of the dying dollar in my jeans
and the junk food possibilities
in the ancient vending machine.

The trucker to my left
farts and almost stifles
his moronic laugh.
I zip up,
stick my hands under the water,
look at the evil vision of my future
in the glass.

So this is my life.

Flat

South Kansas, somewhere on 71
the car's rumble shakes me awake.
This isn't a sound that lulls one back to dreams.
We slow down and coast to the shoulder,
The slow flap of rubber drumming
the pavement. Derek's already
at the trunk, fumbling with the key.
He extracts a bottle jack,
orange and old. I grab the tire iron
from under my seat and exit
the Mustang, stepping into grass
and hoppers, what's left of rain.

We chock with rocks, slide that jack,
lift the car up slow as breath.
Derek holds the tire fast
while I make with the iron
to free the flat and fit the spare,
just too small, meant for short jaunts
across town. When a lug nut bounces
across the road he runs, grabs it, points.
A red-tail lifts from a phone pole
against the dark.

We fit the tiny tire, finish
with the bolts, set that flat
down soft in the trunk. The car
rides like a question back onto the road.
We look quickly for the nearest town.

Come On Down

Someone's kid,
or maybe no one's kid,
is motoring around the
cracked parking lot
in one of those
red and yellow plastic cars
that've been all the rage with toddlers
since Hector was a pup.

The Mustang rolls a little wobbly
with the doughnut riding rim.

Beauty of the modern age;
Rex called in advance from
the comfort of a slightly reclined,
albeit bumpy passenger seat.

I remember a family vacation
when somewhere in
Oklahoma
or Iowa
or Idaho
or some other nowhere,
Dad's panel van blew the passenger rear.
We walked dark highway miles
to the payphone
to hail a tow.

Owner greets us as we exit the Mustang,
offers the "lounge"
complete with network tv—
"We get all three channels,
come in all kinds of clear"—
and a happy abundance
of almost day-old coffee.

Naugahyde seats
cradle our night.

Sometimes they rerun
daytime gameshows
in the post-primetime.
Bob Barker narrates
our schedule's demise.

Sitting in the waiting room,
thick coffee in styrofoam cups
as the 'stang's worked on in the E.R.,
we're implored to:
"Come on down."

Bus Stop

Sometimes the highways
will bring you
right through the middle of town.

Sitting at the red
as the horizon slowly lightens,
red
going on
orange
going on
yellow,
I think about the world,
all those lives.

The shaker hood rattles in time
with my hand on the wheel.

Passenger doses in the
reclined, faded and slashed leather.
Some would wonder how one
could sleep though the rumble,
but I well know,
you get tired enough…

A lean-to of a bus stop to the left,
two elderly men sit on the
rotten wooden bench,
smoke stale cigarettes
and admire our ride.

Forgiving the road dust,
it's still pretty choice from the outside.
If you're not in the know,
you might mistake the dying muffler
for a glasspack.

The light shifts down
and I shift up.

The two at the bus stop
are in our tail lights,
and we're in their past.

South Kansas, Late

The worst part of highways,
lined up like split logs
along the edge: the dead.

Impressionist canvases,
red and black with feathers
or fur and always claws.

When you spit seed shells
or lob trash, you press the gas
and don't look back.

Sometime after Midnight

In a dark highway minute
you can lose yourself.

Especially when you're shotgun,
window down,
invisible black currents
leading your right arm to
dance in the negative space.

Road signs glow alien
in the uneven headlamps.

They proclaim comfortable decadence,
but the rust on the edges,
the foreign air whisper:
keep driving.

The dotted line unravels.

Border Conversation

The clerk's skittish when I approach
the counter to pay our gas tab. I ask. He tells,
nervous, how he'd been held up two days before
at the end of a shift. Oklahoma already feels
different.

He fumbles my change. It clangs
on the counter. He tries to smile, says
we're lucky we came through
today, after shit went south. He says
maybe there'd have been no more
gas stops for us.

I tell him south is where we're
headed. He smiles again, hands me
a scratcher: $2, free. He looks at me.
Maybe you'll get lucky.

Expectations

We roll into this restaurant proclaiming,
"Authentic Mexican Cuisine."
Such claims always seem questionable
when the place obviously
used to be a Waffle House,
and the lady behind the register
looks like she could be
Tammy Faye Baker's
slightly younger sister.

Inside, the hostess does little to
hide that she doesn't want us
(the only patrons thirty minutes before closing)
to be there.

Roles reversed, I wouldn't want
a couple of jerkoffs to wander in
demanding food,
when all I want to do is
get on with real life.

She leads us to a red and white checkered table,
says she'll be back with water, nachos,
and to take our order.

Most of the other tables in the joint
have chairs upended on top of them,
some of the lights in the place are out.

There's shouting from the kitchen,
too muffled to be sure,
but I'm pretty sure it's swearing.

A kid, eight or ten,
comes hauling ass through the dining room,

a sweaty black ball cap in his hand.
A few seconds later,
a man in a stained apron catches the boy,
snatches the hat,
drags the kid by the arm back to the kitchen,
muttering all the way.

Heading into the kitchen,
they pass the woman who seated us.
She brings two glasses of water
and our "nachos."
A plate of potato chips
and a warm bowl of what looks like
aerosol cheese.
For some reason,
this unappetizing appetizer
is the most foreboding part
of the experience so far.

Hand on hip,
not looking either of us in the eye,
sounding kind of accusing,
she asks what we want.

Interior Monologue/Dessert

I.

I've had few nachos that look anything like these.
If I eat these riffle chips and spray cheese,
so joyous yellow the outside sky is made less blue,
I'm fairly certain I may go actually blind.

What I really want: to make good time.
What I want is fuel efficiency. Good faith, too,
in where my food has been and where I am going.
Our waitress, impatient, has forgotten:
When chairs are turned up on tables and the lights
are mainly out does it not make patrons stay longer?

II.

When I bring two dessert mints back to our table
we wipe them clean and open carefully.
They are just slightly stale. The boy shuffles back
into the room; when he tries to take our empty plates
he struggles. They might be heavier than the whole of him.

The apron-wearing man emerges from the kitchen,
takes our plates, tousles the small boy's hair. They smile,
back and forth: the man and this smaller man.
The most authentic people here.

Christ of the Ozarks

They built one in Rio,
I'm told it's pretty impressive.
Pictures I've seen surely
back that claim up.

Somewhere along the way,
these hillfolk decided they
could do it just as good.

Standing in front of the mammoth,
cigarette dangling from lips,
having never seen the original,
I still feel justified in saying
this one missed the mark.

The view's nice, though;
lots of trees and air.

A bird lands on the
plaster man's head,
refreshes the white on the crown.

I spit the butt to the ground,
ask Rex if he thinks
anyone's ever come here,
become overwhelmed with the spirit,
fell to their knees crying.

He shakes his head,
walks off,
like I'm being disrespectful to ask.

I give him a little lead,
then follow,
think about another smoke

before hitting the road again.

I hear they got a
piece of the Berlin Wall
somewhere around here.

Ravenden

By unsaid agreement we head East
out of Eureka Springs. Skirt the Missouri border
for a while, then head South. Perhaps
we'd been nervous to leave the Midwest after all.

It's not a place you'd notice on a map
but I've been here before, at night,
when size is not quite clear. This town
holds less than a thousand people.

Derek parks just off the grass, and we
see it. It looms. Its eyes like small white plates,
a giant raven keeps watch over this little city.
It's daytime, unlike last time.

We get out, touch the dark feathers. It watches
us, I'm sure. We take a photo, then head
south. The highway slowly opens its gray mouth.

Drops

This trip keeps taking us
down weird roads.

Or maybe it's Rex's
unfounded hatred of GPS
that keeps bringing us
to these places.

Not that computers are infallible,
but we, in all our map-reading ability,
surely ain't neither.

Pavement cracked almost to gravel,
traffic signs graffitied to the point
you now know why they made you take
that shape recognition test
to get your DL,
balls-out daylight,
yet guys with open forties and
barely-concealed glocks
lounge on the curb.

A girl no older than five
pedals her trike from the
front of the dilapidated church,
makes it to the middle of the street.

Then her ride drops the front wheel,
it rolls to the gutter,
the girl and the trike stay put.

Show in the windshield,
I slow to a crawl.

The girl gets off the
obviously scavenged banana seat,
proceeds to kick the incomplete trike
with the vitriol of a much older person.

I can't help but laugh and think:
You and me both, kid,
you and me both.

Interior Monologue/Cancer

Bad news always bites. When driving, worse.
No place to sit from shock—you understand,
the car's the only chair you get—your hands
are full of wheel, can't touch you where it hurts.
You have to drive straight on to the next stop,
get out and run your hands through uncombed hair.
No one you know has died today, that's sure,
but the man beside you has had a nasty shock.

He never mentioned his need for this drive
was something you should roll with just because
of his old friend, in the Big Easy, out too far
but slowed—trying to make it through more alive
than going in. But you know the normal laws
just don't apply. You climb back in the car.

Silent Aftermath

We drive in silence for a long while.
Now he knows,
in some rat at the back of the brain way,
I'm sure he always did.

I insisted on driving;
it centers me.
Two and ten,
never-ending pattern of white separated by black
approaching fast,
vanishing behind.
It's constancy,
it's the beautifully terrible reminder
that everything keeps going;
birds and slugs and internal combustion,
it all will keep going
long after
all of our
long-afters.

I sneak a glance to the right,
he's watching the trees
rocket into our past,
but not really;
he digesting,
making sense,
trying to not feel hurt.
I don't blame him,
and I don't know if I've made the right decision.
I could turn around any time,
wouldn't take much to get him home.

I stare out the windshield,
focus on the impossible task
of not thinking about
what this might mean.

Interior Monologue/Passenger

Arkansas

Easy to be overwhelmed. Easy
to wonder why it took this long. Easy
to wonder at motive. Easy
to think of two friends on the road
as just a trip. Easy even to forget
your job teaching about commas
and line breaks and just drive. Harder
to picture what your friend is feeling.
Harder to understand sharp cubes of pain
when you feel only other shapes. Harder
to picture the dread white tile of a hospital
you've never been in. The chemo drip that ticks
away like road lines. Harder to think of this friend
the driver's known longer than you, whose years
ahead will be shorter. Harder to think
of breathing when for some it's
a holiday stocking of small stabs.

Hardest to picture turning back. To
let your friend head south without you.
To breathe without thought while
one state south, blood cells in a bed
unsheathe their knives. So you look
out the passenger window as the trees
tick past. Past. Past.

Goals

These miles keep unwinding,
or stacking up,
or spooling,
or something,
bending into some weird spiral
of distance measured by time,
or perhaps the opposite.

I have to remind myself
to loosen my grip,
relax my shoulders;
there's nothing I can do,
nothing but be there.

Faulty clock in the dash,
green analog lies,
all I know is it's late,
it's dark,
he sleeps reclined
as black landscape
blows past on the other side of glass.

At the bottom of my vision,
knuckles white again,
bone threatening to burst through.

None of this makes sense,
but it was always like this;
endlessly driving to a goal
I never want to reach.

Just Past Midnight

We finally stop
at a roadside motel. I've been here
before, not fleabag exactly, but
the kind you'd recommend to in-laws
if you hated your in-laws.

The room's two beds are rumpled
like someone jumped them,
not on them but like with a knife.
The air wavers. I forgot to ask
for nonsmoking, but Derek doesn't care.
He looks at me, locks
himself in the bathroom.
Probably to think. I sit down
on one bed to wait.

Before morning we have to talk.
I tap in time on the floor
and the clock ticks like trees
past the motel window
and on down the highway, south.

Seat

The lock on the bathroom door
slides into place like the bolt action
on my grandfather's rifle.

I sit on the closed toilet seat,
stare at the overly-noisy exhaust fan
for a long luminescent while.

Sometimes things are too much,
even when you see them coming
from miles — hell, highways — away.

The whole motel smells like
stale cigarettes, but one would guess
every one of the smokes was
burned right here.

After the brush on the highway,
I thought I'd take a break,
but it's not like this place
doesn't already stink like
cheap tobacco and cheaper sex
and no small amount of whiskey puke.

And I need it.
No, I want it, but the want
is brought on by all of this.

By owning up,
by knowing that I don't owe much
of an apology, but I still owe one.
By knowing that whatever I do
and whomever I'm with,
he's still going to die,
and nothing can change that.

The paper feels like home,
the flame is life
and the taste as I suck in the green,
I imagine it's the closest thing
the foliage of Earth can provide us
to unconditional love.

I don't think I'm an addict in the traditional sense,
but life,
life,
life...

Rex doesn't buy into this stuff,
and good on him.

Takes a strong man
to deal with the world unaided.
Most days I want to crawl into a ball,
cry "Mommy,"
and pretend someone will make it all better.

Are you there, God?
It's me, Derek, and as that singer-poet once said:
everything is fucked up as usual.

Someone please tell my friend
in the hospital bed
that I love him.

Tell my friend in the next room the same.
Please tell the world that I love them,
because I can't bear
to open my eyes.

Motel Pool

Even a ripped-felt pool table
can help with pain. The first games
go to Derek. I warm up, not quick enough,
bank some shots, miss them all.
Not on purpose. I don't tell him.

Every shot's like this: you already
explained. Once is enough. For him,
maybe once was too much.
The banks start connecting.

You come shoot pool
to escape new knowledge,
put it off until morning,

until behind the wheel,
where all shots will connect
over the ripped felt of the road.

On the Take

After a few games at the table,
nearly all of which were
too one-sided to be anything other
than at least somewhat staged,
I coax Rex to the hotel bar
(or at least what passes for one here)
before they close up shop.

The man behind the counter
that was obviously built for something else,
he's got one job:
trade booze for cash.
Not that hard,
but he-of-the-pasty-bald-spot
and sunken eyes
curls lips back from yellowed teeth
in an ill-tempered grimace,
only at the last minute switching gears,
morphing his face into a smile.
It's not even a little convincing.

Rex goes for a generic beer,
but at least it's a tallboy,
I opt for a double
bourbon and Coke.
I want to ask for a triple,
but that feels wrong for this place.

After setting our drinks in front of us,
the bartender makes for the back room.
Rex takes a short pull from his beer,
I down a third of my icy brown concoction
in one go.

We sit in silence,

he making like he's studying the letters on his can,
me watching the room in the smudged mirror behind the bar.

Eventually he asks,
"Want to talk about it?"

I think hard, then sigh,
  "No. Not really."

Rex straightens up to face me.
"You know we're going to have to talk eventually."

I don't make eye contact.
"Yeah. Not tonight, though."

We return to silence and finish our drinks.
The bartender never comes back to collect.
It'll end up on the bill for the room,
I'm sure.

Nothing is free.
Everyone pays.

Everyone always pays,
and everyone keeps on paying
until they can't pay anymore.

Sooner or later,
we all run out,
but that won't stop
the world's greedy hands.

4:15

The air is humid and stale,
the AC is some warble of hell,
and here we are.

I pick up my phone,
stretching the cord from the wall;
almost an hour-and-a-half
since last time I checked.
I'm not sure how long
I was awake before the
first time I checked.

Back when I was a kid,
back when everything
always seemed so important,
if I ever complained about
lying awake at night,
Dad would always ask,
"What'd you do wrong?"

It's that greybeard voice now
flying bomber drills
around my conscience,
my unwanted consciousness.

I didn't do a damn thing wrong.

But maybe I did.
It's so hard to tell these days;
the older I get,
the more life happens,
or happens to me,
or doesn't happen to me,
that line that once seemed
so sharp,

so perfect,
so undeniable,
so final,
it's become increasingly blurry;
a faded stain on a tablecloth,
an idea, not a directive,
a goddamned serving suggestion.

I know I don't always make
all the right decisions,
but I know on some
unconceitedly base level,
that my heart shouldn't be
racing with this poison guilt.

I look at the phone again.

4:15.

I'm going to have to drive soon.

Toward the End

of the dream I've had
nine times before, the bleak room
with the tall marble pillars
is suddenly and certainly the lobby
of a train station. No tracks but silence,
no light but a soft blue bubble,
the kind made by soap, levering
through the black air toward me.

In slow motion, it begins to rupture.
Light from nowhere plays
across the folding surface of the soap.

It bursts like an accordion.
Just before Derek shakes my shoulder
to wake me, the trains thunder
through the wall.

I dress in silence.
Derek takes back the key,
returns with coffee. We
leave the darkness for the car.
The morning's gray advances
slowly to the road.

Marker

Sometimes you drive in silence;
the best thing you can say
is nothing.

As I'd lain awake,
wishing for sleep,
but really only waiting for
the moment to move,
it was obvious something heavy
was going on in Rex's world.

Everyone's got their demons,
but it's odd how sometimes
you just assume certain people don't,
until they're in your face
and you can't deny them.

We haven't spoken a word.
His eyes haven't left his
passenger window.
The sunrise is a foggy non-entity today.
Why are we doing this?
What good could possibly come?

I downshift.
Maybe there's some answers
after the next mile marker.

Drive

Verb. To press something forward
into motion, maybe yourself. This comes laden
with assumptions about reason. Why the need
for motion at all? What makes one
expend one's life to drive something?

Noun. Internal call to motion,
if that motion is intentional.
Not just why we get up
in the morning. Often a deeper
sense of purpose, not always
articulated. Importantly
when experiencing *drive*
you must be okay with that.

Lights

I'm pretty sure
it used to be a sedan.

One of the few good things
about dark drives
in the middle of zero space
at that special time when no one,
not even the earth itself
is moving in any meaningful way:
no rubbernecking when there's
some crushed-to-nothing
vehicle leaking what's left of itself
onto the crumbling shoulder.

The ambulance is there,
flashing its radioactive warning
into the clouded night sky.

Rex slows,
we crawl past,
as if driving a little slower
really makes any of this safer.

There's a filled-out and zipped-up
body bag on a stretcher
situated in the negative space
between the shredded car
and the ambulance that's
now obviously shouting to
save no one.

Those lights blinking in the mirror,
we leave that death behind,
just so we can barrel into another one.

Is life what happens in between deaths?

Storm Warning

We're getting low on gas again
in the just-post-evening static
when the first signs begin to appear.
The windows are down, and the rain
when it begins is warm. Not long
before we have to crank them up. We see
how others have the same idea:
trucks and vans ahead snap on their taillights.
Derek's arms tighten slightly against
the building wind. Water splashes
down harder to the craggy road.

I check the glovebox for flashlight,
batteries, map. He tells me
in the trunk we have a jack, spare tire,
bottled water, blankets, flares.
We are at least a bit prepared.
He begins to look ahead of us
into the gathering dark for exit signs.

Small white birds begin to pass
above the car on their opposite way,
their small voices Dopplering astray
before the storm.

Drill

Rex rummages, finds what we got;
what we got's good enough
to keep us alive if we need,
but it's not much.

Long-haul truckers are turning back,
taking cues from birds,
but I'm determined to plow through this,
drill a fucking hole through that black
that's threatening to swallow
everything in front of us.

If this darkness wants me,
it can take me.
Maybe this is what it comes to,
maybe it's always been
coming to this.

Rex looks uneasy in his
shotgun seat to Armageddon,
can't say I blame him;
I know how this must look.

Everything in me says:
grip that wheel tighter,
floor it,
suck in that breath big,
'cause it might be the last,
but it just might be the first.

News

An hour past dark.
Derek comes back to the car
at the single unbagged pump.
The tank is full. He hangs up,
looks at me, pockets his phone.

*They don't think he'll last
the night,* he says. The hospital.
I don't press further. Derek stares
into the windshield where droplets
race and vanish in the wipers.

Curtains of rain whip down.
We ease over to the street
where the lights blink yellow
down the rippling pavement.
All is beginning to flood.

Wet

We ride in silence.
The cacophonous rain
does all the talking.
Drops on the hood manage
to be both
maddening and comforting.

If nothing else,
there's small solace in the
consistency of life's annoyances.

Earlier, before the
gas station,
before the phone,
radio said we wouldn't
get through — road flooded,
impassable.

Lightning ahead and behind,
backlighting the storm,
this night,
this failure.

Any other way would take us
so far out, he'd be gone
long before we walked
through the door.

Rex looks ahead,
knowing just as well as me
we'll soon be turning around.

It was all pointless,
everything always is.

Futile battles seem to be
my specialty, so we keep on
to an inevitable dead end.

The rain keeps falling.

Eventually,
we all get soaked.

Return Ghazal

For some people dreams begin with a car.
For others: the road just ahead of the car.

For the driver beside me: it let him pretend
that a promise could travel and so could his car.

Thunder ahead of us, preparing to shout,
can cut off the voice from the mouth of a car.

Rain sweeping the road in the treads of our wheels
has trimmed short the threads of the plan for this car.

We'll return, and you'll ask us, but what did you feel?
A road, an idea, nothing else but a car.

Notes

JB: A lot of the places and situations in my poems are pulled from my life. The Mexican diners, the rest stops, the endless highway miles, the small children on scavenged trikes on cracked inner city streets, the old men at bus stops. They're all out there. Go find them.

TRS: Many of the circumstances depicted in my poems were inspired by actual happenings and places as well. For instance, Ravenden, Arkansas really does have a giant, spooky raven statue that seems to peer right through your soul—it's just near the edge of town. Similarly, the narrative's car trip is a composite inspired by events from many different journeys, some taken by James and some by me. And Louisiana really does flood like crazy.

About the Authors

James Benger (Derek) is a father, husband and writer. His work has been featured in several publications. He is a member of the Riverfront Readings Committee, and is on the Board of Directors of The Writers Place in Kansas City. He is the founder of the *365 Poems in 365 Days* online poetry workshop and is Editor In Chief of the subsequent anthology series. He lives in Kansas City with his wife and children. Read his work at jamesbenger.wordpress.com .

"Sometime After Midnight" was published in I-70 Review. 2018.
"Drops" was published in "Little Fires Hiding" with Jason Baldinger, 2018.

Tyler Robert Sheldon's (Rex) books include the poetry collection *Driving Together* (Meadowlark Books, 2018) and the chapbook *Consolation Prize* (Finishing Line, 2018). He received the 2016 Charles E. Walton Essay Award and is a Pushcart Prize nominee. His poetry, fiction, and reviews have appeared in *The Los Angeles Review, The Midwest Quarterly, Pleiades, The Dead Mule School of Southern Literature,* and other venues. Sheldon currently is an MFA candidate at McNeese State University. He lives in Baton Rouge and is married to the artist Alexandria Arceneaux. Read his work at TylerRobertSheldon.com .

www.ingramcontent.com/pod-product-compliance
Lightning Source LLC
Chambersburg PA
CBHW030134100526
44591CB00009B/648